BITCOIN

The Absolute Beginner's Guide to Bitcoin Cryptocurrency and how it will change your finances now and beyond.

BY Smith, Luk Brandon

Introduction:

Bitcoin has been the trendy expression in the monetary space. Starting at a self-evident reality, Bitcoin has detonated the scene over the most recent couple of years and numerous people and numerous huge organizations are currently getting on board with the Bitcoin or cryptographic money trend needing a slice of the pie. People, who are completely new to the digital money space are continually posing this inquiry; what is bitcoin truly?

Indeed, first off bitcoin is digital money that falls outside the control of any government, it's utilized around the world, and can be utilized to buy things like your food, your refreshments, land, vehicles, and different things.

Bitcoin isn't vulnerable to things like legislative control and vacillations in the unfamiliar monetary standards. Bitcoin is sponsored by the full confidence of (you) the person and it's stringently distributed. This implies anybody completes exchanges with Bitcoin, the main thing they understand is that it's significantly less expensive to use than attempting to send currency from one bank to another or utilizing some other administrations out there that require sending and accepting currency universally.

The customary type of currency will in general lose its value with the progression of time given a few components, like swelling. So, advanced money is a type of speculation. Most kinds of money include a fixed period upon the formation of new coins. Then again, you can make a currency account without giving person subtleties as long as you would prefer not to profit by assistance that requests person subtleties.

Furthermore, the beauty of the framework is that it offers a 100% acknowledgment rate. You should simply open the digital currency site on your PC or cell phone and afterward make the record. You don't need to go to the workplace of an organization for account creation. Inside a couple of moments, the record will be made.

Chapter 1 - Learn About the Benefits of Bitcoin

Bitcoin is decentralized digital money that is claimed by none. Government has no power over it. It utilizes distributed systems administration and cryptographic evidence to work the system. The system is controlled and made misrepresentation free by accounting exchanges in blockchain, a public history account, whenever they are approved with a proof of work system.

The organization started working in 2009 and is an idea including virtual money which has no connection to government-managed currency. The Bitcoin system enjoys not many benefits like:

- It is more affordable to work and utilize this virtual currency.
- Like different monetary standards, the amount of this virtual currency is fixed and nobody has the option to make new Bitcoins. However, people can mine Bitcoins however there is a cutoff to it and mining Bitcoins isn't at all modest.
- Bitcoin is free money; no association has any power over it
- It is a majority rule of money.
- As it utilizes an advanced medium, it can turn out to be considerably more significant than gold.
- It is what might be compared to something of significant value.

More about Bitcoins

Bitcoin is a graphic of the genuine innovation in play. These coins address the actual currency and are the ones executed. They are sent or gotten through wallet programming running on a PC, a web application, or a cell phone. They can be acquired through product and services trades, or mining.

What is Mining?

Mining is essentially the interaction through which new bitcoins are made. For each exchange that happens, accounts are kept consecutively in a public information base called the blockchain. The people who keep up this blockchain are the diggers, and their prize is recently made bitcoins.

Utilizing Bitcoins

These coins can undoubtedly be gotten for various monetary forms. The easiest path is to buy them for currency. Some organizations stretch out the trade administrations to their clients with rates being controlled by such factors as volume.

Some people have put resources into bitcoins, with the assumption that their value will rise. While this believability is verifiable, it conveys some danger with it. This along with certain characteristic constraints like the irreversibility of the exchanges, the instability of the Bitcoin swapping scale, and the restricted client attentiveness make contributing a hold to just the complex financial backers. On the potential gain, however, Bitcoin can bypass expansion, making it ideal for regions where public monetary standards are dangerous.

The Future of these Coins

A few financial experts declare that this innovation has offered digital money that has for a long time ago been wanted. Others have thought that it was less convincing, contending that its absence of dependability and its unpredictability are debilitating. In any case, numerous shippers have gotten used to it, and its developing notoriety suggests that its prosperity as a standard method for payment is impending.

In case you're new to Bitcoin and invest a lot of your energy on the internet, you should check it out. It offers a variety of adaptability and accommodation that is absent in other accessible payment doors.

Learn About Bitcoin Conveniently

You can find out about Bitcoin from different sources on the internet. You can check sites, magazines, books, and so forth Web is a generally excellent hotspot for a beginner to study Bitcoin. Through web journals and discussions, you'll learn specialized, financial, and policy-driven issues identified with the Bitcoin system. These mediums are a rich wellspring of data and you can learn everything about this virtual currency.

Besides, regardless of whether you are now in the system and know a considerable amount about how it functions, you can remain refreshed on each news and issue about the new digital money system. It's likewise astute to get enlisted on related gatherings and start conversations with the specialists. Post strings and get some information about.

This is the best learning source as you get profited from other's experience. The advanced arrangement of Bitcoin money appears to be convoluted to the people who think nothing about it and a great many people discover the idea difficult to handle and trust. It won't take some time before people begin tolerating and afterward receiving this virtual currency system, which is safer, open, and free.

Contrasts among Bitcoin and customary monetary Bitcoin doesn't have a concentrated power or clearing house (for example government, national bank, MasterCard, or Visa organization). The distributed payment network is overseen by clients and diggers throughout the planet. The money is namelessly moved straightforwardly between clients through the internet without going through a clearinghouse. This implies that exchange charges are a lot lower.

There is a restricted measure of Bitcoins available for use. The trouble to mine Bitcoins (address calculations) gets more enthusiastically as more Bitcoins are created, and the greatest sum available for use is covered at 21 million. The breaking point won't be reached until around the year 2140. This makes Bitcoins more significant as more people use them.

Bitcoin is made through an interaction called "Bitcoin mining". Diggers throughout the planet use mining programming and PCs to settle complex bitcoin calculations and to support Bitcoin exchanges. They are granted exchange charges and new Bitcoins produced from settling Bitcoin calculations.

Bitcoins are not guaranteed and are not insured by government organizations. Henceforth, they can't be recuperated if the mysterious keys are taken by a programmer or lost to a flopped hard drive, or because of the conclusion of a Bitcoin trade. If the mysterious keys are lost, the related Bitcoins can't be recuperated and would be unavailable for general use.

Advanced money is acknowledged by a set number of dealers on the internet and in some physical retailers.

The digital currency can be obtained through Bitcoin mining or Bitcoin trades.

I accept that Bitcoin will acquire acknowledgment from the public since clients can stay mysterious while purchasing labor and products on the internet, exchanges charges are a lot lower than MasterCard payment organizations; the public account is available by anybody, which can be utilized to forestall extortion; the currency supply is covered at 21 million.

Contemplating whether you should put resources into Bitcoin?

If you've been around any sort of monetary news recently, you've presumably found out about the fleeting ascent on the planet's most notable digital currency. Furthermore, in case you're similar to many people directly about now, you're most likely pondering, "Bitcoin - yes or no?" Should you contribute? Is it a decent alternative? Also, what the hell is Bitcoin at any rate? Here are few things you should keep in mind about Bitcoin before you contribute. Also, note that this book is for data purposes just and ought not to be taken as any sort of monetary guidance.

It utilizes an innovation called blockchain, and many people have been posing the inquiry "What is blockchain?" So permit me to expound a piece. The blockchain network is an open account that shows every exchange that is made, and is honest because there is nobody's area where every one of the accounts is kept. This forestalls any digital assailant from ruining the data on the account.

This is the fantasy that was thought out by its maker because the ascent of bitcoin and blockchain was made out of the doubt from the banks and monetary foundations during the lodging emergency of 2008. So the possibility that each hub (PC) on the organization could see and check each exchange that is being made, achieves a type of trust.

This digital financial system has opened entryways for another approach to go through with exchanges over the Internet. Particularly for dim web clients who use cryptographic money to purchase malignant things like weapons, medications, and assassins. The persistent utilization of bitcoin for buying labor and products over the internet is the thing that gives it its force as I would like to think.

Pros of Bitcoin

- **Restricted Supply**

There are 21 million Bitcoins that can be mined. This restricts the measure of Bitcoin that can at any point be delivered. This resembles saying an administration can't print currency because there is a restricted inventory of bills - and they will not print any longer. When there is a set stockpile your buying power is protected and the money is invulnerable to rampant expansion. This restricted stock has also assisted with adding to the ascent in the cost of Bitcoin. People don't need money that can be printed - or swelled - into endlessness at the impulse of a ravenous government.

- **Less expensive to Transact**

Numerous organizations want MasterCard these days. Notwithstanding, these cards remove some somewhat generous charges from every business exchange. Yet, a shipper who acknowledges Bitcoin doesn't pay these weighty charges - so it places more currency in their pockets. So those are a portion of the fundamental experts of Bitcoins.

- **Simple to Send Money**

Since it's decentralized, this likewise implies that you can send a companion Bitcoin (currency) on the opposite side of the world in seconds without going through a bank delegate (and pay the financial expenses). This reality alone makes Bitcoin mainstream. Rather than sitting tight for a wire move which can require days, you can send your payment right away or in minutes.

- **Private**

A great many people imagine that Bitcoin is mysterious. However, it's not mysterious - it's more private. All Bitcoin exchanges at any point made can be seen on the Blockchain - the public Bitcoin account.

Every exchange is connected to a location - a line of text and characters. So while people may see your location - it's impossible to connect that address to you. Many people who don't care for their banks keeping an eye on them (or revealing to them the amount of their currency that they can or can't move), truly like this protection highlight.

- **Dangerous - Price Fluctuations**

Bitcoin is acclaimed for rising gradually over months - and afterward falling 20 - half a few days. Since it's being exchanged 24 hours daily. And everything necessary is some terrible information - like the information on the Mt Gox hack a couple of years prior - to send the value tumbling down. So, essentially it's not steady - and there are a lot of questions out there that can influence the cost. The standard here is this: don't place any currency into Bitcoin that you can't bear to lose.

- **Bitcoin Transactions Not Reversible**

Not at all like a MasterCard charge, Bitcoin exchanges are not reversible. So if you send Bitcoin to some unacceptable location - you can't get it back. Likewise, there is a lot of stories from people who have lost their Bitcoin wallet address and they've lost their coins. It is extremely unlikely to get them back.

Consequently, you truly need to understand what you're doing and save time to explore how to purchase and store your coins appropriately if you need to put resources into Bitcoins - or some other digital currency.

- **Easing back Transaction Speeds**

Bitcoin is beginning to run into higher exchange expenses. Other digital currencies have gone along that is quicker and less expensive. The Bitcoin diggers are dealing with the issue. However, until these issues are settled, you can anticipate that the price should be very unpredictable.

So those are a portion of what to consider before putting resources into Bitcoin. Essentially, while Bitcoin has a lot of incredible things making it work - and keeping in mind that it can change monetary exchanges as far as we might be concerned - there is still a lot of dangers. There are a lot of questions out there still. If you do choose to purchase, take as much time as necessary and examine your choices. Try not to purchase from simply any dealer. Some of them are reliable and maintained an extraordinary business. However, others will cheat you and may not convey your coins.

The Future of Currency Is Digital

Would we be in an ideal situation without paper currency and coin? Some say indeed, and some say no and the discussion seethes on. Government charge gatherers would lean toward just electronic or advanced currency - it's simpler to control and simpler to keep citizens legitimate - however, are those additions value the downsides?

There are the unlawful things, nobody utilizes digital currency since it leaves a follow, so you can't utilize it to purchase things you are not permitted to purchase or that another person isn't permitted to sell.

Does it accordingly, bode well to dispose of the currency that permits illicit exchanges, shut down the whole underground economy, and if we do, will our general public and civilization be better or more regrettable off for that arrangement? How about we examine this, will we? Indeed, an advanced currency would be like normal money and truly we are nearly there as of now at any rate.

If we go to "digital units" and change the worldview to cover the requirements of people who contribute who are not compensated decently now, then we will get a greater amount of what we reward, similar to the acclaimed maxim. A technocrat would appreciate this discussion and the prospect of miniature dealing with the specific value of each work, yet technocrats are not all that great at considering their own made unanticipated outcomes as they clear the way to hellfire.

The explanation people use currency presently is essential that things and decisions are more muddled than they were in the past when our species were just trackers, finders, and brokers. Allow me to clarify; you see, if I make sleds and you need one, however you just have steers, then, you can't remove the tail of your cow to purchase my mallet, so you give me $11 and you can sell your cow later on for $1100 and give me its one-percent so you can assemble another animal dwelling place.

Bitcoin: All It's Overvalued Up to Be?

The dispatch of Bitcoin prospects on December tenth, which interestingly will permit financial backers to enter the Bitcoin market through a significantly directed US trade, infers that we are simply beginning. There will just at any point be a limit of 21 million Bitcoins and not at all like ordinary fiat monetary forms, you can't simply print a greater amount of them at whatever point you feel like.

This is because Bitcoin runs on a proof of work convention: to make it, you have to mine it utilizing PC preparing ability to tackle complex calculations on the Bitcoin blockchain. Whenever this is accomplished, you are compensated with Bitcoin as payment for the "work" you have done.

Lamentably, the award you get for mining has diminished pretty much consistently since Bitcoin's beginning, which implies that for the vast majority the solitary suitable approach to get Bitcoin is by getting it on a trade. At the current value, levels are that a danger value taking?

For the people who don't have the foggiest idea, the internet site bubble was a period between 1997-2001 where numerous web organizations were established and given absurdly idealistic valuations dependent on theory that later dove 80-90% as the air pocket fell in the mid-2000s. A few organizations, for example, eBay and Amazon recuperated and now sit far over those valuations however for other people, it was the stopping point.

Bitcoin was initially made to remove influence from our monetary systems and put people in charge of their currency, removing the center man and empowering distributed exchanges.

Like any resource, when there is more popular to purchase than to sell, the cost goes up. This is awful because these new financial backers are entering the market without comprehension blockchain and the fundamental standards of these monetary forms meaning they are probably going to get singed".

Another explanation is that Bitcoin is very unstable, it has been known to swing up or down a great many dollars in under brief which if you are not used to nor anticipating it, makes less experienced financial backers alarm sell, bringing about a misfortune. This is one more explanation Bitcoin will battle to be received as a type of payment.

This sporadic development can clear out their whole benefit. Will this insecurity disappear any time soon? Not likely: Bitcoin is a moderately new resource class and although awareness is expanding, just an exceptionally little level of the total populace holds Bitcoin. Until it turns out to be all the more generally conveyed and its liquidity improves essentially, the instability will proceed.

So, if Bitcoin is futile as genuine money, what are its applications? Many trust Bitcoin has proceeded onward from being a practical type of payment to turn into a store of significant value. Bitcoin resembles "digital gold" and will essentially be utilized as a benchmark for other digital forms of money and blockchain activities to be estimated against and exchanged for.

Already, there have been accounts of people in high swelling nations, for example, Zimbabwe purchasing Bitcoin to clutch what abundance they have instead of seeing its value decrease under the wildness of its focal financial system.

If you put stock in how these cryptographic forms of money will help the world, it is never past the point where it is possible to get included, yet with the expense of Bitcoin being so high is it a boat for some which have effectively cruised.

It is maybe unavoidable that this sort of advanced, shared, money would rise, yet it is the defects in the current systems that are giving it a lift. As people lose confidence in the public authority and banks, they will be searching for something that will give more alternatives.

They will see the benefits of skirting the broker of MasterCard. Global exchanges will begin to end up skirting the mediators of banks and wire administrations.

As public monetary standards destabilize, they will begin to see electronic, non-public, money as a decent save currency to fence against expansion, runs, and so on Due to the maltreatments in our present system, Bitcoin has created force. That energy is transforming into a show fate. That predetermination is that it will have its spot close by public monetary standards as this present reality hold money.

This money, when it arrives at a minimum amount, won't be effortlessly controlled by people or governments. It will allow us an opportunity, not an assurance, but rather a possibility, to address the system.

The Reality of Bitcoin

I'm a judgment matchmaking master that composes frequently. Bitcoin is a payment system dependent on an exclusive type of digital token currency. Bitcoin is a dealing system that is an option in contrast to paying with currency, checks, PayPal, or MasterCard.

Bitcoin has numerous inconveniences, including:

A portion of Bitcoin's advantages may have problematic value. The promoted benefits incorporate having the option to email your companion's currency, it is identified with gold, it offers protection and strength, and so on The issue is, currency, checks, MasterCard, prepaid currency cards, currency orders, trading with something (e.g., postage stamps), wire moves, and PayPal; appear to cover pretty much every payment need.

Although Bitcoin has its charms, it is exclusive and isn't essential for, or sponsored by any administration. Just a limited number of Bitcoins have been made, which helps cause Bitcoins to appear to be more important than they are. By restricting the number of coins made, joined with the promotion, has pushed up the cost of Bitcoins.

Purchasing Bitcoins isn't modest. Furthermore, aside from EBay, purchasing Bitcoins isn't basic or simple; and except (presumably) eBay, a portion of the Bitcoin merchants appear to be somewhat flaky.

In my tests, the product to make a Bitcoin "wallet" on your PC appeared to be moderate and carriage. I tried two distinctive Bitcoin wallet projects, and it appeared as though they would have required days to complete the process of organizing things with Bitcoin's far-off worker organization.

With Bitcoin, the odds of getting ripped off for buys endlessly increment, because no merchant data is imparted to the purchaser, like their name and address.

I would figure that because Bitcoins are thoroughly secure and private, and because they can be utilized to purchase anything anyplace, utilizing them may help get you on the public authority's radar.

I may not be right, and maybe Bitcoin use will develop, and more Bitcoins will be given, and it will get standard on cell phones, and be acknowledged by pretty much every regular store, for instance, Amazon and Apple. At this moment, the approaches to pay for Amazon buys with

Bitcoins Crime

Regardless of whether you think bitcoins are the currency of things to come or a passing trick, you can't reject that a few people have effectively made millions. So with the fascination of "simple" currency comes wrongdoing. What's more, the wrongdoing is getting greater and more modern.

It disintegrates the trust in the system and is normal. Most web insightful people realize how to stay away from the most exceedingly awful of it. Since Bitcoins are as yet restricted for the most part to geeks, it has been even to a lesser degree an issue. Destinations immediately jumped up that accounted confided in merchants, purchasers, and locales just as those not to work with. The system was self-policing quite expeditiously.

Since the stakes have been raised, we have a lot more elevated level danger to the Bitcoins system. The Bitcoins wallet is presently put away in a typical registry and is decoded. So anybody with admittance to your PC can "take" your Bitcoins very quickly. The infection searches for that catalog and ships the data to the crook.

People downloaded it to check whether it helped and were tainted. Regularly this is something that not very many of us would readily do. Yet, in the Bitcoins world, everybody was taking a stab at a benefit. Time was packed as people seized each an open door in this "dash for unheard of wealth" sort of climate.

Toward the beginning of June, a person lost $500,000 value of Bitcoins to this technique. The person had downloaded a few things and didn't know when or how the Trojan was introduced. He tracked down a couple of malware things when he ran an infection check. The Trojan was without a doubt welcomed into his PC and seeing as how Bitcoins are so new an infection programming would be probably not going to need to ensure the Bitcoins wallet.

The exchange was seen on the Bitcoins organization and an unidentified person posted about their fruitful wrongdoing on Twitter. People have required the Bitcoins people group to gather as one and opposite the exchange. The inclination is this would make a risky point of reference as to what other exchange could then be turned around. Who demonstrates that a genuine offense was submitted? As of the composition of this, the currency has not been recuperated.

By and by Bitcoins and Bitcoins clients are figuring out how to adjust. The most recent adaptation of the Bitcoins programming will scramble the wallet behind a secret phrase. Once more, people are distinguishing which programming and applications are protected and which ones are not. The system is self-revising once more.

Huge currency and the new press for Bitcoins will carry the upsetting side of the trade to Bitcoins over and over yet with all the figuring power and mechanical expertise that is in the current Bitcoins people group, I question that variation will be extremely a long way behind.

What You Need to Know About Acquiring and Owning Bitcoins?

Bitcoin systems are monetary forms that were made in the year 2009. They are digital coins that are sent using the internet. The exchanges are frequently made without go-betweens, like banks. Moreover, the exchanges are worked with no exchange expenses and dealers don't need to give their names. Today, numerous traders are starting to acknowledge the system. Therefore, you can purchase anything utilizing the system from pizza to web facilitating administrations and even nail treatments.

Decentralized money

The systems are the principal perceived decentralized monetary standards and today they are a limited number, with 21 million anticipated to be available in the market until 2140. The system's esteems are continually fluctuating. Consequently, the system's specialized examination is needed to realize the best ideal opportunity to purchase and sell the currency. Right now, there are numerous online money trades where financial backers can trade Euros, dollars, pounds, and different monetary forms. It very well may be exchanged through Bitcoin merchants, just as Forex representatives. Subsequently, it is prudent to look for merchants to get an incentive for your currency.

Why exchange Bitcoins?

The system can be used to purchase stock secretly. Besides, worldwide payments are modest and simple since they are not bound to a solitary country nor are they exposed to the guideline. More modest organizations are especially intrigued by the system since MasterCard expenses are nonexistent. A few groups purchase the system to put resources into with the expectation that their value will go up.

Albeit each exchange is appropriately accounted in broad daylight logs, the names of the merchants and purchasers are rarely uncovered. The solitary way they are distinguished is by using their wallet IDs. That assists with keeping client exchanges hidden.

Getting Bitcoins

The system can be gained by essentially purchasing at a trade. There are a few trades that permit people to sell or purchase the system utilizing various monetary standards. The move is another method of procuring it, where people send it to others utilizing versatile applications or PCs. A circumstance that is like sending currency carefully.

Mining offers another method of securing the system, where people contend to "mine" for it utilizing PCs for motivations behind tackling complex numerical riddles. Today, champs are getting remunerated with around 25 Bitcoins at regular intervals.

Is the Bitcoin an Alternative to Fiat Currency?

As of late, there has been a great deal of talk about another virtual money considered Bitcoin that is becoming quickly, it's acquiring a lot of media consideration and its value has expanded significantly. The current monetary unrest in Europe and throughout the planet has also caused people to put resources into options in contrast to fiat currency like Bitcoin. For the vast majority, it is bizarre that somebody can treat appropriately money that isn't upheld by a Government or focal establishment, yet that is the exact benefit of this coin.

Bitcoin is an extremely intriguing idea that is acquiring acknowledgment by numerous organizations on the internet. A portion of the pundits of Bitcoins say that they are working with purchasing drugs on the internet, the designers say that virtual money is only a device and you can utilize it for fortunate or unfortunate.

Fiat currency has the hindrance that focal establishments can print however much they need; in this way it is continually losing buying power. A similar rule applies if you have currency in the bank. Rather what you should do is put your currency on a resource that keeps its value or increment it. Already, Bitcoin appears to be a decent choice since it's expanding its value, however, this can change later on. Another option is to put your currency in something useful like a business or land that expansions in esteem or put it in gold.

Although virtual currency is a decent method to expand your portfolio and not rely upon paper currency or bank stores, you need to search for an approach to store a value that is secure against the monetary fence and the most ideal choice is Gold, since it's definitive currency. Gold has been a store of significant value for quite a long time and will consistently be, because it's important, it's restricted in amount, it's simply replaceable, and it's a store of significant value.

Getting Gold Bullion with Bitcoin

It is simpler than you might suspect. I figured out how to find a quite certain approach to utilize my bitcoin to purchase gold bullion every month on robotization.

The following steps are included to make this a triumph:

- Begin mining bitcoin
- Connection your online wallet with a visa card
- Set aside bitcoin and purchase gold bullion
- Begin organizing and allude people to your technique
- Procure subsidiary commissions
- Begin mining bitcoin

If you are inexperienced with bitcoin, help yourselves out and begin investigating this digital currency that is utilized all through the entire world presently. It is changing our method of living rapidly and will keep on doing as such. I have investigated the bitcoin market and found a route to mine bitcoin on the internet and get paid every day, without agonizing over any equipment support, power expenses, or sharp decreases in your benefit.

There are a lot of detriments to claim bitcoin equipment, because of the significant expenses of power to run the gear. In this way, what you should do as the absolute initial step, get an agreement with a bitcoin mining organization that is trusted and exist. There are so numerous Ponzi plots out there that you should be on high ready constantly.

Connection your online wallet with a visa card

Whenever you have tracked down a legitimate organization, begin mining bitcoin and send it to your online wallet to store as much bitcoin as possible inside a brief period. Search for a bitcoin wallet organization that offers their customers a visa card that can be connected to their wallet.

Save bitcoin and purchase gold bullion

This card would then be able to be utilized to make buys web-based, drawing currency at a bank, or simplifying payments like purchasing goods. Every one of the exchanges is simply bitcoin that you are spending and none of it is coming from your real ledger. When you have the visa card you would be in a situation to buy gold bullion on the internet.

The subsequent stage is to discover an organization that sells gold bullion on the internet and you would have the option to pay for it utilizing your MasterCard. Utilize the visa card I referenced before in this book and get some gold bullion. To begin with, test the system and guarantee that the gold you purchase is 24 karat gold. I would suggest you purchase your gold bullion in 5-gram pieces as they are simpler to work with when required.

Begin organizing and allude people to your technique

There are various approaches to make decent pay and one of them is utilizing the force of systems administration. Whenever you have figured out how to grasp your piece of gold bullion by buying it with bitcoin, people would need to know how you did it.

Procure associate commissions

If you have chosen organizations inside the bitcoin and gold bullion market that offer their customers a member commission, you would acquire an incredible easy revenue from your systems administration endeavors. This is only a portion of the strategies I use to assemble an online business that I know would keep going for quite a long time to come.

Bitcoin is a progressive kind of money that was presented in 2009. It capacities by empowering exchanges to go through without the requirement for the center man. Hence, no banks are required. You likewise get the advantage of no exchange expenses and no compelling reason to give out your genuine name. With such adaptability, bitcoin has gotten broadly acknowledged by the two shoppers and traders.

It also can be utilized to buy web facilitating services, food varieties on the web, and pretty much any help, you can consider on the web. Bitcoin has affected much on the money field. It very well may be handily used to buy stock namelessly. It also gives the advantages of simple and modest worldwide installments and isn't oppressed or restricted to any country or guideline.

A few groups consider Bitcoin to be a vehicle for speculations and purchase Bitcoin by believing that it will increment in esteem. To get Bitcoins, you can buy them on an Exchange commercial center that permits people to purchase or sell them, using other different monetary forms. The moving of Bitcoins is effectively done by sending Bitcoins to each other person using portable applications or their PCs on the web. It's similar to sending currency carefully.

With Bitcoins, you have money esteem that can be store in what's known as a "digital wallet," which remains alive either inside the cloud or on a PC. This advanced wallet resembles a virtual ledger that lets account holders inside it send or get Bitcoins, buy labor and products or store them.

Albeit most ledgers are protected by the FDIC, Bitcoin wallets are not, yet they are protected, secure, and have installment adaptability benefits. In contrast to the US dollar, gold, silver, or some other valuable metals, Bitcoins are scant and this shortage is algorithmic. As far as the worldwide settlement, Bitcoin is a victor. There is no stress over misrepresentation or security. At some currency trade organizations, for example, transient laborers could use Bitcoin to send installments starting with one country then onto the next through email.

On the 27th of June in 2014, the US Government was booked to unload around 30,000 BTC that was seized from the closure of Silk Road, an online underground market activity. Around then, the value of Bitcoins was 633.84 dollars. Today, one Bitcoin is valued at about $655.48 US dollars. If you investigate a portion of the nearby traders' downtown, downtown areas, or on the web, you will see the Bitcoin logo acknowledgment in the window or on the entryway. Bitcoin is as yet developing and is making a gigantic movement towards being perhaps the most reasonable monetary form at any point made.

What Are a Cryptocurrency and Bitcoin?

The Web is significant for any society. It is formed by the society. Furthermore, until society is an error-free zone, the Web will not be an error-free zone. So what is cryptographic money? Cryptographic money is a decentralized installment system, which fundamentally allows people to send currency to one another ridiculous without the requirement for a confided-in outsider like a bank or monetary organization. The exchanges are modest, and by and large, they're free. Furthermore, the installments are pseudo unknown also.

That well, the fundamental element is that it's completely decentralized, which implies that there's no single essential issue of power or anything like that. The ramifications of this are finished by everybody having a full duplicate of the relative multitude of exchanges that have at any point occurred with Bitcoin. This makes a staggeringly strong organization, which implies that nobody can change or opposite or police any of the exchanges.

The significant degree of obscurity in there implies that it's exceptionally difficult to follow exchanges. It's not unimaginable, but rather it's unfeasible by and large. So wrongdoing with digital currency - because you have quick, borderless exchanges, and you have an undeniable degree of secrecy, it in principle makes a system that is ready for abuse.

So much of the time when it's an error on the web with online installment systems. Various organizations are investigating Bitcoin and taking a gander at Bitcoin and attempting to see how it functions and how they can deal with police it.

It's likewise been in the media on many occasions, and the media, being the media, similar to zero in on its terrible side. So assuming there's a burglary or a trick or something to that effect, they will in general pin it on Bitcoin and Bitcoin clients. So the most remarkable is presumably Silk Road, which got brought down as of late, and through their $1.2 billion value of Bitcoins, went to pay for anything from medications to firearms to hit men to such things. What's more, the media, once more, rapidly put this on Bitcoins and say that it was the Bitcoin client's shortcoming.

So, there's in reality almost no proof of the size of the issue of wrongdoing with digital forms of money. We couldn't say whether there's a great deal or we couldn't say whether there's a bit. However, people rush to mark it as something criminal, and they fail to remember the real uses, like quick and fast installment.

So a couple of exploration addresses I'm taking a gander at in this space is what does wrongdoing with Bitcoin resemble? So many people will say that tricks and burglaries have been continuing for a very long time. Yet, the methods through which they happen to change with the innovation.

So a Victorian road backstabber would essentially be doing something different to a 419 Nigerian ruler con artist. So the following inquiry that I'd prefer to investigate too is taking a gander at the size of the issue of wrongdoing with digital currency. So by producing a log of known tricks and robberies and things like that, we would then be able to cross-reference that with the public exchange log, everything being equal, and see exactly the amount of the exchanges are unlawful and criminal.

Anyway, how much does the actual innovation work with wrongdoing? By glancing back at the wrongdoing logs, we can see which specific kinds of wrongdoing occur and if it is really the innovation's issue or is this simply the normal, worn-out violations that we've been taking a gander at previously. What's more, whenever we've thought about these things, we can begin to consider potential answers for the issue of wrongdoing with Bitcoin.

Does Bitcoin Make Good Sense?

Most specialists will highlight the ascent of bitcoin. Bitcoin is on the ascent of digital money utilized around the world. It is a kind of currency controlled and store altogether by PCs spread across the Internet. More people and more organizations are beginning to use it. Dissimilar to a plain U.S. dollar or Euro, bitcoin is likewise a type of installment system similar to PayPal or a MasterCard organization.

From numerous points of view, bitcoin is something beyond currency. It's a re-designing of a worldwide account. It can break down hindrances among nations and liberates currency from the control of central governments. So, it depends on the U.S. dollar for its value.

Bitcoin is constrained by open-source programming. It works as per the laws of science, and by people who altogether direct this product. The product runs on a lot of machines around the world, yet it very well may be changed.

Changes can happen anyway when most of those supervising the product consent to it. The bitcoin programming system was worked by software engineers around five years prior and delivered onto the Internet. It was intended to stumble into a big organization of machines called bitcoin diggers.

This dispersed programming produced the new currency, making few bitcoins. Fundamentally, bitcoins are simply long advanced addresses and equilibriums, store in an online record called the "blockchain." But the system configuration empowered the money to gradually extend and to urge bitcoin diggers to keep the actual system developing.

When the system makes new bitcoins, it offers them to the diggers. Diggers monitor all the bitcoin exchanges and add them to the blockchain record. In return, they get the advantage of granting themselves a couple of extra bitcoins. At present, 25 bitcoins are paid out to the world's excavators around six times each hour. Those rates can change over the long run.

Diggers watch bitcoin exchanges through electronic keys. If they don't make any sense, an excavator can dismiss the exchange. Once upon a time, you could do bitcoin mining on your home PC. However, as the cost of bitcoins has shot up, the mining game has transformed into somewhat of a space race.

Today, the entirety of the PCs competing for those 25 bitcoins perform 5 quintillion numerical estimations each second. What's more, mining can be quite dangerous. Organizations that form these custom machines commonly charge you for the equipment forthright, and consistently you hang tight for conveyance is a day when it gets more diligently to mine bitcoins. That diminishes the measure of currency you can acquire.

For what reason do these bitcoins have esteem? It's quite straightforward. They've developed into something that many people need and they're in the restricted stockpile. Although the system keeps on putting out bitcoins, this will stop when it arrives at 21 million, which was intended to occur in about the year 2140. Bitcoin has entranced numerous in the tech local area.

So, if you follow the financial exchange, you know the value of a bitcoin can vary extraordinarily.

A more reasonable view recommends that examiners will at last reason bitcoin to crash. It doesn't fuse the capacity to use its currency in the retail climate, apparently an unquestionable requirement for long-haul achievement. Its wild variances likewise make it a tremendous danger for speculation purposes. However, bitcoin pushes the limits of innovation advancement. Similar to PayPal in its earliest stages, the commercial center should choose if the danger related to this kind of advanced money and installment system makes for great long-haul negotiating prudence.

5 Merits of Bitcoins

A lot of people have known about the term Bitcoin however don't have an unmistakable thought of what it truly is. Characterized, Bitcoin is a decentralized, distributed, digital currency system, intended to enable online clients to deal with exchanges using an advanced unit of trade known as Bitcoins. All in all, it is a virtual currency.

A private organization of PCs associated with a common program is utilized to complete exchanges and interaction installments in Bitcoin. The making of Bitcoins depends on progressively complex numerical calculations and its buy is made with standard public currency monetary forms.

Clients of Bitcoin can get to their coins with their cell phones or PCs. As another and developing the virtual currency, Bitcoin enjoys certain unmistakable upper hands over ordinary government-level monetary standards. Here are 5 best advantages of utilizing Bitcoin.

Adaptable Online Payments

Bitcoin is an online installment system and like some other such system, the clients of Bitcoin have the advantage of paying for their coins from any side of the world that has a web association. This implies that you could be lying on your bed and buying coins as opposed to taking the agony of making a trip to a particular bank or store to complete your work.

Also, online installment through Bitcoin doesn't expect you to fill in insights concerning your data.

No Taxation

When you make buys using dollars, euros, or some other government fiat currency, you need to pay an extra amount of currency to the public authority as an assessment. This is considered an authoritative document of tax avoidance and is one of the significant benefits of being a Bitcoin client. With zero expense rates, Bitcoin can prove to be useful particularly when buying extravagance things that are elite to an unfamiliar land. Such things, as a rule, are intensely burdened by the public authority.

Negligible Transaction Fees

Bitcoin isn't checked or directed by any go-between establishment or government office. Accordingly, the expenses of executing are kept extremely low dissimilar to worldwide exchanges made using ordinary monetary standards. Furthermore, exchanges in Bitcoin are not known to be tedious since it doesn't include the inconveniences of ordinary approval prerequisites and holding up periods.

No External Mediations

Perhaps the best benefit of Bitcoin is that it wipes out outsider interferences. This implies that legislatures, banks, and other monetary mediators have no authority at all to disturb client exchanges or freeze a Bitcoin account. As referenced previously, Bitcoin depends rigorously on a distributed situation. Thus, the clients of Bitcoin appreciate more noteworthy freedom when causing buys with Bitcoins than they do when utilizing regular public monetary forms.

Disguised User Identity

All Bitcoin exchanges are discrete, or all in all, Bitcoin gives you the alternative of User obscurity. Bitcoins are like money just buys as in your exchanges can never be followed back to you and these buys are never associated with your personality.

Indeed, the Bitcoin address that is made for client buys is never something similar for two distinct exchanges. If you need to, you do have the choice of deliberately uncovering and distributing your Bitcoin exchanges yet by and large clients keep quiet.

Advanced monetary standards, for example, Bitcoin are similarly new and haven't yet been put through significant tests. Thus, many feel that there are sure dangers implied in the use of Bitcoin. However, the expected disservices of Bitcoin, it's obvious that its benefits are sufficiently able to make it a real competitor to challenge regular monetary forms not long from now.

Would You Be Able to Make Money from Bitcoin?

Over the most recent half-year, we have seen the cost go from $20 a coin in February, up to $260 a coin in April, back down to $60 in March, and back up to $130 in May. The cost has now settled to around $100 a Bitcoin, however, what occurs next is impossible to say. Bitcoin's future eventually lays on two significant factors: its appropriation as money by a wide crowd, and the shortfall of restrictive Government intercession.

The Bitcoin people group is developing quickly, interest in Cryptocurrency has spread significantly on the web, and new services are tolerating Bitcoin installments progressively. Writing for a blog monster, WordPress acknowledges Bitcoin installments.

We have effectively seen people make millions on the currency. We are seeing expanding quantities of people trying different things with living just on Bitcoin for quite a long time while recording the experience for narrative review. You can purchase a takeaway in Boston, espresso in London, and surprisingly a couple of vehicles on Craigslist utilizing Bitcoin.

Looks for Bitcoin have soared in 2013, with April's climb and ensuing fall in the Bitcoin cost. A week ago the principal huge procurement of a Bitcoin organization was made for SatoshiDice, a web-based betting website, for 126,315 BTC (about $11.47 million), by an undisclosed purchaser.

This quick development in mindfulness and take-up looks set to proceed if trust in the currency stays solid. Which prompts the subsequent reliance. Unofficial law. Albeit explicitly intended to work freely from Government control, Bitcoin will unavoidably be influenced by Governments here and there. This should be the situation for two reasons.

Initially, to accomplish undeniable degrees of reception, Bitcoin should be available to huge quantities of people, and that implies spreading past the domains of covered up exchanges to ordinary regular exchanges for people and organizations. Also, these Bitcoin exchanges could turn into an identifiable piece of people's available riches, to be pronounced and controlled close by some other kind of abundance.

The European Union has effectively proclaimed that Bitcoin isn't classed as a Fiat currency, or as currency, and thusly, won't be directed by its own doing. In the US, the 50 state system and various regulatory bodies included have settled on choices more troublesome, with no agreement arrived at so far.

Bitcoin isn't viewed as currency accordingly, yet it is considered to go about as currency. A flourishing Bitcoin market in the US has a more dubious future for the time being, and any indisputable enactment in the US could either have an extremely sure, or an exceptionally adverse consequence on the eventual fate of Bitcoin.

Bitcoin network is possibly the world's tremendous spread processing project. Bitcoin wallet documents can get lost, taken, or erased incidentally very much like some other records in digital structure. So, clients can utilize sound security procedures to ensure their money. On the other hand, you could pick the specialist organizations that offer significant level security, just as protection against misfortune or robbery.

Why Bitcoin Remains Volatile Option for Investors?

For the people who have not been following the adventure of Cryptocurrency, Bitcoin, and Litecoin, it might come as unexpected that monetary standards with no characteristic value stay an unpredictable ware for financial backers. For the people who have been staying aware of transformation rates for digital currency, unmistakably the very instability that has characterized pseudo-money is the thing that is keeping financial backers keen on this field.

Ongoing changes in the value of such currency just as chapter 11 of perhaps the greatest stage on the planet trading Bitcoins has raised doubt about the fate of this advanced currency. Nonetheless, specialists console the people who need to utilize Crypto Currency, Litecoin, and Bitcoin that the "prevailing fashion" that prompted digital currency is likely digging in for the long haul.

A Short History of Bitcoin, Cryptocurrency, and Litecoin

Bitcoin and different types of pseudo-money are utilized as installments for exchange charges, items, and services. Bitcoins or Litecoins can be traded for "genuine" money at a given rate. Specialists were worried that Bitcoins and other digital currency may be utilized for criminal behavior as they are a lot simpler to trade and "launder" than different types of currency.

The value of these monetary standards has also been the subject of discussion. Bitcoin esteems rose 90-overlay in 2013, making a "Bitcoin bubble" that emptied rapidly in 2014. The unexpected drop in esteem by around 50% has prompted the theory that the pseudo-money field is passing on and before long will go the method of the dodo.

So, is it too early to proclaim Bitcoin and Litecoin a disappointment? Specialists differ regarding the matter, however in some cases that there is a spot in the upcoming monetary market for advanced money.

We generally required an approach to exchange esteem and the most commonsense approach to do it is to interface it with currency. Previously, it functioned admirably because the currency that was given was connected to gold. So, every national bank needed to have sufficient gold to repay all the currency is given.

However, in the previous century, this changed, and gold isn't the thing that is offering value to currency however guarantees. As you can get it's not difficult to manhandle such force and positively the significant national banks are not denying to do as such.

Hence, they are printing currency, so all in all, they are "making abundance" out of nowhere without truly having it. This cycle not just opens us to the dangers of a financial breakdown yet results also in the downgrading of currency. Subsequently, because the currency is useless, whoever is selling something needs to build the cost of merchandise to mirror their genuine value, this is called swelling. In any case, what's behind the currency printing? For what reason are national banks doing as such? Indeed, the appropriate response they would give you is that by debasing their money they are helping the fares.

In reasonableness, in our worldwide economy, this is valid. In any case, that isn't the solitary explanation. By giving new currency we can bear to take care of the obligations we had, as such, we make new obligations to pay the old ones. However, that isn't just it, by downgrading our monetary standards we are accepted de-esteeming our obligations.

That is the reason our nations love swelling. In inflationary conditions, it's simpler to develop because obligations are modest. However, what is the results of this? It's difficult to store abundance. So if you keep the currency (you endeavored to get) in your ledger you are losing abundance because your currency is cheapening before long.

Since every national bank has an expansion focus of around 2% we can well say that keeping currency costs we all at any rate 2% each year. This debilitates savers and prods utilization. This is the way our economies are working, in light of expansion and obligations.

What might be said about collapse? Well, this is by and large something contrary to swelling and it is the greatest bad dream for our national banks, how about we see why. Fundamentally, we have to empty when generally the costs of products fall. This would be brought about by an expansion in the value of the currency.

Most importantly, it would hurt spending as customers will be boosted to set aside currency because their value will increment over the long haul. Then again, traders will be feeling the squeeze.

They should sell their merchandise rapidly else they will lose currency as the value they will charge for their services will drop over the long run. Yet, if there is something we scholarly in these years is that national banks and governments couldn't care fewer customers or traders, what they care about the most is DEBT.

In a deflationary climate, the obligation will turn into a genuine weight as it will just get greater after some time.

Since our economies depend on the obligation you can envision what will be the outcomes of emptying.

So to sum up, swelling is development amicable however depends on obligation. In this manner, people in the future will pay our obligations. Collapse then again makes development harder however it suggests that people in the future will not have a lot of obligation to pay.

Is Bitcoin Money?

What is currency? Currency is an estimation unit with the end goal of trade. Currency is utilized for the valuation of merchandise, settling obligations, representing work performed, and normalizing the estimation of creation. Currency must be separable, versatile, stable in esteem, simple to acquire, sturdy over the long haul, and should be trusted by all gatherings utilizing it.

Envision the currency that is too huge to even consider separating into pieces, weighty to convey, ruins following 2 days, gets harmed effectively, or can be eaten by creatures? If these are the attributes of the money, it would not be that helpful and numerous agreements would not occur.

The main component of currency is trust. If you work for somebody and you don't know whether you will get paid, would you take every necessary step? If you took the necessary steps and got paid for something that was not acknowledged in numerous spots, is it a legitimate installment? The economy and currency system are based on trust, and it tends to be broken by an absence of trust by most people.

A sudden spike in demand for a bank is an exemplary illustration of people losing trust in a bank and it failing presently. Trust is likewise the zenith of exchange and agreements. If you don't accept the person whom you are doing trade with is reliable, the arrangement would not be started. Security is a component of trust.

If each arrangement you made was communicated in the public domain, a segment of trust would be lost. Somebody may undermine your agreement or deny you of the returns after the arrangement is finished. The best security is accomplished through protection. If somebody realizes you have raked in boatloads of currency, they will figure out how to take it from you if that is their goal.

On account of bitcoin, does it work as currency? It is compact, effectively separable, can be utilized to esteem resources and settle obligations. Is the value stable? Since the cost of Bitcoin moves around a ton versus different monetary forms, the appropriate response is likely no. If you are attempting to purchase a crate of apples and are paying for them in Bitcoin, those apples can twofold in cost in seven days, then go down 30% the following week, and afterward twofold in cost presently.

If each exchange was this unstable, you would not have the option to purchase numerous merchandise and skill much you can spend. The same thing would occur with business bargains. The cost of the entirety of the parts would change fiercely and make a ton of issues in making bargains because the expenses and incomes would shift excessively.

Is Bitcoin dependable? Trust can be seen from various perspectives. In the conventional currency systems, the value of money is being dissolved by expansion. One way of thinking faults it on higher work, material, and overhead expenses over the long run - creation contributions for business. Another way of thinking says that swelling is a financial wonder, which implies that whoever gives the currency is giving more currency than the products being delivered. Is swelling a genuine attribute of currency or is it a lethargic robbery over the long run?

If you don't believe how the currency system functions, you may put more trust in Bitcoin since it is decentralized. The issue with decentralized systems is: Who will cover for misrepresentation, tricks, or terrible conduct? The controller or focal position goes about as the ref to keep the game clean.

If the arbitrator is paid off or is one-sided, in any case, abruptly the trust is lost and the game should be played without a ref if the actual players are straightforward. If your bitcoin wallet is lost or your passwords lost, you won't get to your bitcoins by the same token.

Alternate ways trust can be addressed incorporate having restricted admittance to currency (capital controls or system breakdown if advanced money), parting with quite a bit of your currency to an outsider (tax collection, coordinated wrongdoing, or maybe mint piece excavators and trade administrators), fake currency (physical or digital), wholesale fraud or loss of trust in a guarantor (insolvency). Bitcoin is a competitor to be money, however, the strength of cost and trust for the normal person has not been set up yet.

Alright, so how this fits with bitcoins?

However, bitcoins are intended to be an option for currency and to be both a store of significant value and methods for exchanging merchandise. They are restricted in number and we won't ever have more than 21 million bitcoins around. Subsequently, they are intended to be deflationary. Presently we have all seen what the results of collapse are. So, in a bitcoin-based future, it would, in any case, be workable for organizations to flourish.

The best approach will be to change from an obligation-based economy to an offer-based economy. Indeed, because contracting obligations in bitcoins would be pricey organizations can, in any case, acquire the capital they need by giving portions of their organization. This could be an intriguing option as it will offer numerous venture openings and the abundance created will be appropriated all the more equally among people.

However, only for clearness, I need to say that piece of the expenses of getting capital will be diminished under bitcoins because the charges would be amazingly low and there will not be delegates between exchanges (banks rip people off, the two borrowers, and moneylenders). This would cradle a portion of the negative sides of collapse. By the by, bitcoins will deal with numerous issues, sadly, as governments need fiat currency to repay the colossal obligations that we acquired from the past ages.

Variables to Consider When Choosing a Bitcoin Exchange

Bitcoin isn't different from a PC program or a portable application that gives a person a wallet, permitting clients to send and get Bitcoins. Even though there are numerous trades accessible for people looking for a chance to exchange or put resources into BTC, information on how the system works are basic before beginning. The way toward moving currency over trade can be a thorough interaction.

It is difficult to secure, which clarifies why it is essential to include Bitcoin dealers or trades. The way toward tracking down a dealer or trade is more than discovering one with the most attractive site. The components to consider while picking a trade include:

Closeness

Bitcoin remains a moderately unregulated currency, albeit the scene is required to change in the long haul. There is more openness by monetary enterprises and media in such a manner. We will encounter more governments needing to apply some power over how money-related value is communicated. This is ascribed to the public authority's need to check and keep the instrument from being utilized for criminal operations, for example, tax evasion, illicit medication pirating, and illegal intimidation. Given the distinction in costs, it is imperative to confirm the geographic area of any trade. Moreover, the area of the trade will direct to financial backers and dealers what laws they need to follow.

Liquidity

It is exchanged a market where merchants and financial backers are searching for a chance to sell or purchase the currency. In this way, it is fitting to consider the liquidity a trade has. The term liquidity alludes to the capacity to sell a resource without the costs being influenced essentially, thus making the costs drop. The absolute biggest trades offer high selling costs, which thusly makes an impact that permits the system to produce into a big organization where more people can join.

Expenses

Purchasing and selling do include currency. The currency is preferably the motivation for the specialists or trade. Regardless, in contrast to purchasing securities or stocks, Bitcoin trades charge a rate, while markdown representatives utilized by most financial backers charge level rate expenses. The rate model, buying, and selling over the long run can demonstrate costly. A portion of the famous trades charges higher rate expenses based on a sliding scale, given volume. Henceforth, they charge less rate where more volumes have been exchanged inside a time of thirty days.

Should Real Estate Wholesalers Accept Bitcoin?

Bitcoin is hot. So should financial backers wholesaling properties be scrambling to acknowledge bitcoins or is it another significant entanglement to stay away from?

The buzz about bitcoins appears to just be developing, similarly as the virtual money is soaring in esteem. So what are the genuine advantages and disadvantages of managing this advanced money for those wholesaling houses? Is it an unquestionable requirement to have or should keep away from? There are numerous advantages of fusing bitcoins into business for those wholesaling properties.

This incorporates:

- Making it simpler for additional people to purchase from and contribute with you
- Cashing in on the sensational expansion in bitcoin cost
- Attention from educated financial backers and purchasers
- Increased press, brand availability, and viral spread

On the brilliant side, those that have followed this news will know that this all had little to do with utilizing bitcoins, and everything to do with the criminal operations being purchased and sold. Indeed, the way that the public authority is allegedly selling the advanced coins it swiped makes bitcoin genuine.

It's getting simple to acknowledge bitcoin, and the sky is the limit from there, and more organizations in different businesses are receiving it. At this moment there is a stunning open door for depending on the accomplishments of the money and press by taking it.

For some, it very well may be their best advertising move of the year and truly help to dispatch their organizations to a higher level. This will not be an entryway of chance open for long. We are talking many months before the curiosity wears off and everybody is doing it.

There are some basic contemplations to remember, however. Many may favor spending and tolerating bitcoins for security. Nonetheless, while Bitcoin Magazine reports 90% of those in presence are being accumulated, there is the potential for huge changes.

Throughout the most recent year, this has worked in the blessing of bitcoin proprietors and diggers. Coins that valued only a couple, or two or three hundred dollars a year prior are presently exchanging for hundreds and a huge number of dollars. Because of the set number of people holding them, there is a ton of control in a couple of hands. To perceive the benefit of utilizing them in wholesaling properties, however, consider the outcomes of holding a lot in virtual currency.

Would It Be a Good Idea for Me to Invest in Bitcoin?

In recent months, I have watched bitcoin's value ascent dramatically. With the new government and media consideration, digital currencies have gotten, they have stood out enough to be noticed.

Digital money or all the more advanced currency is acquiring acknowledgment rapidly everywhere in the world as it makes exchanges speedier and less expensive. These exchanges are gotten by cryptography and every exchange has its signature or private key. With its ascent in value and notoriety, everybody needs a slice of the pie. There are two fundamental approaches to bring in currency with bitcoin.

The first is a lovely clear technique for buying the coin as a venture and expectation that its value increments. The second is the way toward "mining" bitcoins. When an exchange has happened they are then confirmed over the organization by "excavators" utilizing muddled calculations. As an award for their work, they get exchange charges and also newly printed bitcoins.

From a contributing stance, there is a major danger/reward factor as this currency is moderately new and has no inherent value causing instability and large value changes. A positive certainty is that there is a tremendous measure of currency put resources into this and organizations are marking on to utilize this money so we have no clue about when its value will return to nothing.

"Mining" likewise has a major danger/reward factor. Toward the start of bitcoin, you used to have the option to "mine" with a customary PC or home PC. So, presently as more people are doing it the trouble and force are expected to "mine" increments. Bitcoins have a most extreme sum that can be stamped (21 million).

Furthermore, as we draw nearer and more like 21 million the measure of bitcoins compensated for each effective "mine" gets more modest and more modest. Presently "diggers" seeming to be productive need to put resources into confounded innovative mining apparatuses and there is still no assurance they will be beneficial or even make their expenses back.

In any abrupt happening that guarantees wealth the most worthwhile endeavor is selling the instrument that helps produce this wealth. For instance, in a dash for unheard of wealth, it would be the digging tool and in "mining" for bitcoin, it would mine apparatuses or incredible realistic cards. If you can deliver these or even get your hands on some modest, you would make an impressive benefit flipping them. Lamentably, just a chosen handful has the advantage of picking this alternative. With people rushing towards the wealth hanging before them the trick specialists are having a field day also.

Benefits of Choosing a Bitcoin Mixing Service

Today, people from everywhere the world are utilizing this help without offering their data to the world. In any case, if you want to profit from the help straightforwardly from the stage Bitcoin itself, you need to alter your perspective. For obscurity, you need to utilize a solid Bitcoin blending service. If this seems as though something new to you, we can assist you with getting it.

Benefits of a Bitcoin Mixing Service

If you decide to pay to utilize advanced currency, you will not need to pay any charges. Essentially, it's imperative to take note that these exchanges are not mysterious. This is a big data set of these exchanges, which implies your data is imparted to the person you are managing.

The motivation behind the assistance is to work with the proprietors. Accordingly, if you utilize this assistance, you don't need to enlist by giving your data. If you are a first-time client, you can look over the variety of services that will not charge you anything. Similarly, they will not need the PGP key confirmation. However, the reason for the services is to guarantee that you appreciate genuine namelessness when making these exchanges.

Since there is a great deal of interest in these blending services, con artists are exploiting the system to bring in currency. Hence, it's significant that you get your work done before picking a decent blending service. Tracking down a dependable supplier is of genuine significance.

What you need to do is recruit a blending service that will not request your name, email, or other personal data. Likewise, the specialist organization shouldn't track exchanges their clients make consistently.

Nobody controls virtual money as it tends to be gotten to by the general population on the internet and the value keeps on appreciating while the general public staggers on the garbage of swelling.

A conventional man on the roads can purchase, save, exchange, contribute and increment his odds of getting monetarily effective without the impedance of government limitations, controls, and trustee guidelines; consequently, winding swellings become relics of times gone by. Numerous accept the number 1 issue in our general public is setting up monetary restraining infrastructures. When one enterprise chooses to control unfamiliar trade, gold, and fuel, it utilizes its influence to direct how currency s should have spent.

Guidelines set by huge and affluent multi-organizations are simply equipped to add more riches and influence to their portfolio as opposed to profiting borrowers who look for monetary assistance. Also, the ones at the top attempt to clean out the badland so others can rely upon them while they can get richer yet they can't handle advanced currency.

Conclusion:

Bitcoins have become a very notable and famous type of currency over the long haul. However, what precisely is Bitcoin? The book will go over through this currency that sprung up out of nowhere and spread out of control. What makes it unique about ordinary monetary forms? Bitcoin is advanced currency, it isn't printed and never will be. They are alleged electronically.

They are delivered by people and organizations, making the first historically speaking type of currency known as a digital currency. While ordinary monetary standards are found in reality, Bitcoin goes through billions of PCs from one side of the planet to the other. Bitcoin is founded on unadulterated math. It has nothing to cover up either as it's open-source. So, anybody can investigate it to check whether it's running how they guarantee.

All through our lifetime, we've seen numerous progressions happen from how we shop, how we watch films, how we tune in to music, read books, purchase vehicles, search for homes, presently how we go through currency and banking. Cryptographic money is staying put. If you haven't as of now, it's the ideal opportunity for anybody to completely contemplate digital currency and figure out how to exploit this pattern that will keep on flourishing all through time.

Lightning Source UK Ltd.
Milton Keynes UK
UKHW050943100621
385112UK00021B/436